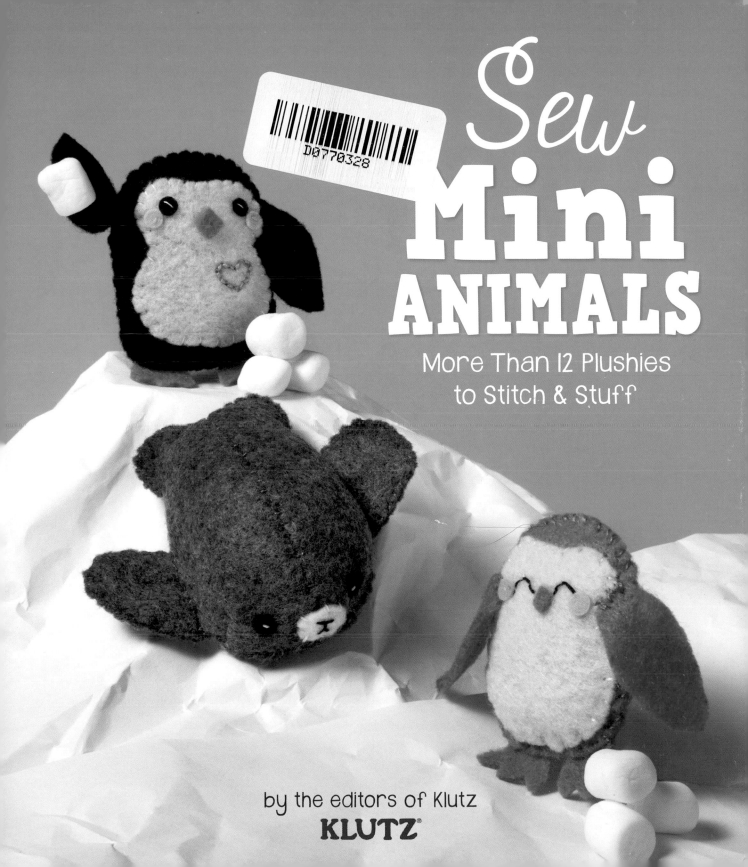

Sew Mini ANIMALS

More Than 12 Plushies to Stitch & Stuff

by the editors of Klutz

KLUTZ®

CONTENTS

What YOU GET

9 colors
of felt

Stuffing

Traceable patterns

2 embroidery needles with holder

30 pre-cut eyes and 30 pre-cut cheeks

8 colors of embroidery floss

Other stuff you'll need:
Scissors
(small, sharp blades to cut felt)
Optional:
Ribbon, ruler, thimble, pen

START HERE

Learn the basic skills you'll need to sew all of your animals by completing the penguin before you move on.

PENGUIN

This sweet little guy is a wonderful way to start your training as a Mini Animals maker!

Almost every project will use a needle, eyes, cheeks, a small handful of stuffing, a pen, and scissors, so keep those handy. For the patterns, floss, and felt you need, check the field guide. Here's what you need for the penguin:

FIELD GUIDE

Supplies:
- Black floss
- Cream floss
- Orange floss
- Pink floss

Trace and Cut:

 x2

2 penguin bodies

1 penguin belly

 x2

2 penguin wings

1 penguin beak

 x2

2 penguin feet

TRACING

You'll find patterns in the box that will help you make all of the animals in this book.

(1) Take the penguin front pattern and place it on top of a piece of cream felt. Lay it very close to the edges to get the most out of the felt without wasting too much.

(2) Take a pen and trace around the pattern.

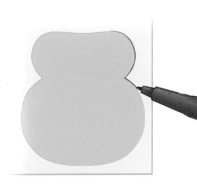

(3) Do the same for the two penguin feet and one penguin beak on orange felt.

WILD TIPS

If you will need two pieces that are irregularly shaped (like the bat wings on page 23), flip the pattern over before tracing the second one, so the wrong sides will be back to back.

For dark colors, like the black you need for the penguin, see Step 3 on the next page.

CUTTING

You'll need sharp, small scissors to snip the felt in clean lines. Go slow, and watch your fingers.

1 Using sharp scissors, very carefully cut along the lines you traced for your penguin belly. When you are done, one side might have lines or marks from tracing on it. That's called the "wrong side" of the felt.

2 Cut out the penguin feet and beak in the same way.

WILD
TIPS
Turn the felt, not the scissors, to cut corners and curves.

3 With dark-colored felt, like black, you won't be able to see your pen marks. Instead, carefully pin or hold the pattern against the felt and cut around it. Try this method to cut out the penguin body and wings.

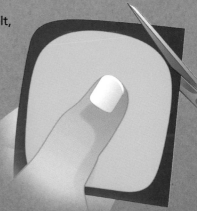

USING FLOSS

Embroidery floss usually has six strands wound together. For the projects in this book, you'll only need two strands at a time. Here's how to separate them.

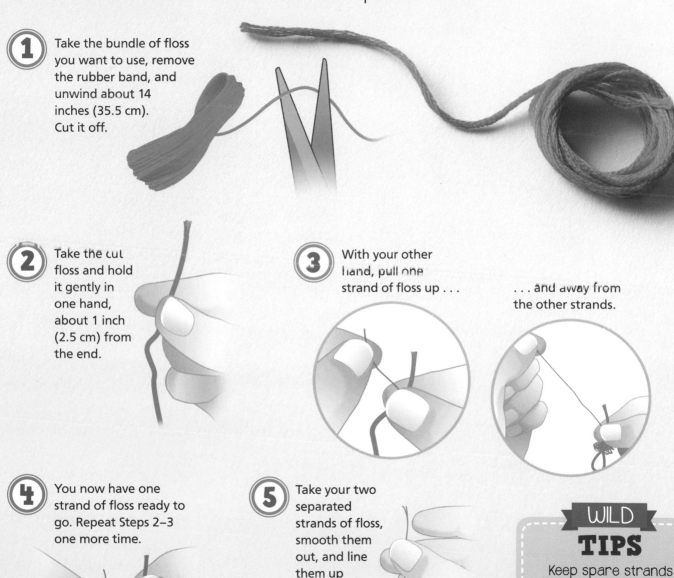

1 Take the bundle of floss you want to use, remove the rubber band, and unwind about 14 inches (35.5 cm). Cut it off.

2 Take the cut floss and hold it gently in one hand, about 1 inch (2.5 cm) from the end.

3 With your other hand, pull one strand of floss up . . . . . . and away from the other strands.

4 You now have one strand of floss ready to go. Repeat Steps 2–3 one more time.

5 Take your two separated strands of floss, smooth them out, and line them up together.

WILD TIPS

Keep spare strands of floss loose and untangled, so you can use them later for another project.

Threading
THE NEEDLE

1 Trim the ends of your two strands so they're even and free of fuzz.

2 Moisten one end and pinch the strands together so they're nice and pointy.

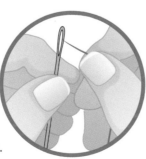

3 Poke the moistened end through the hole in the needle (this is called the eye). Now pull your floss through until you have about 4 inches (10 cm) past the eye.

SAFETY ✕ STUFF

★ Always handle needles with care. Don't rush the stitches.

★ Needles are sharp. If you have a thimble, wear it to protect your fingertips while stitching.

★ Keep needles away from small children, pets, and bare feet.

★ Store your needles when you're finished working. You can use the needle holder provided, or a storage unit of your choice.

★ If a needle breaks, carefully check the surrounding area and throw out broken needle pieces.

★ If a needle breaks the skin, gently clean the area and apply a bandage. Get an adult to help you.

★ These animals are for decoration only. Do not give them to small children to play with.

★ If finished projects get dirty, spot-clean them with a damp rag and warm water. Do not wash the felt in a washing machine.

Tying a
STARTING KNOT

French Knot

1 After threading you should have one short end and one longer end of floss hanging through the eye of the needle.

2 Place the needle tip near the end of the long piece of floss, and wrap it around three times.

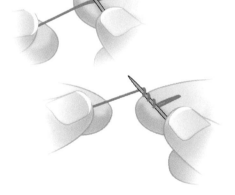

3 Pull the needle up while holding the wraps in place with your other hand.

WILD
TIPS
If you are having trouble mastering this French Knot, any knot you tie near the end of the long strand will work just fine.

Finishing
FLOSS

French Knot

1 When you're done adding details, turn the felt over so that you're looking at the wrong side. Poke the needle under one of the nearby stitches (not through the felt) to create a loop.

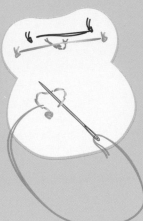

2 Wrap the end of the floss around your needle two or three times.

3 Pull the needle until a knot forms near your felt. Cut your floss close to this knot. Your floss is now secure!

If you find this too hard, or if your floss isn't long enough, try this:

- Take the needle off of your two strands of floss.
- Separate the strands.
- Twist one around the other and pull them tight. Do this a couple of times until it feels secure.
- Cut the floss close to the knot.

ADDING FACES

Putting the eyes on first helps you line up the rest of the face.

Eyes &
CHEEKS

1 Place the eyes on the penguin front, about ¼ inch (0.6 cm) from the top and side edges.

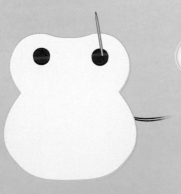

2 Using a needle with black floss, poke up through the back of your felt and through the eye.

3 Poke your needle back through the other side of the eye and finish your floss (page 12). Repeat Steps 2–3 to attach the second eye.

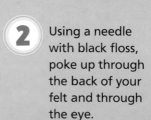

Eyelashes can be added to fancy things up.

For winking eyes, stitch a small sideways "v" using a back stitch (page 14).

4 Use cream floss to make two small stitches in the middle of each eye for maximum cuteness.

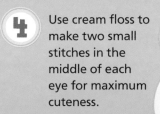

5 For the penguin, the beak (orange floss) and cheeks (pink floss) are attached the same way, with one small stitch each.

ADDING DETAILS

Back Stitch

With a smile or a frown, making a mouth is the final step to the most fun animal faces. The penguin doesn't have a mouth, but back stitch can also make cute details like a chin or a heart.

1 Poke your needle up through the back of the felt and pull the floss until the starting knot just touches the back. Now poke your needle through the front of the felt to make one very small stitch.

2 Poke your needle up through the back again, one stitch length away from your first stitch.

WILD
TIPS
If you are doing a detail like a heart, you might want to draw it lightly on the felt first. But it is best to do it without drawing if you can, because the ink might show through.

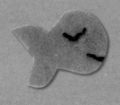

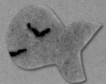

16

3 Now you'll do something a little different: Poke your needle into the ending hole of the last stitch you made and then poke it back out one stitch length past your starting point.

4 Pull your floss all the way through until it lies flat without puckering. That's one back stitch!

5 Continue repeating Steps 3–4 until you reach the end of your design. Poke back through the felt one more time, so your needle is at the back, then finish your floss (page 12).

Your penguin's personality is starting to show! Now it's time to assemble the rest of the body using whip stitch.

Attaching the
FRONT TO THE BODY

Whip Stitch

1 Thread your needle with two strands of cream floss (page 9). Lay the penguin belly facing up on the "right side" of one of the penguin bodies. Make sure it is centered.

2 Poke your needle up through the back of the penguin body just outside the edge of the belly. Pull the floss all the way through.

3 Poke your needle back down about ⅛ inch (0.3 cm), crossing the edge of the penguin front. Pull the needle through to make one whip stitch.

4 Keep on stitching this way until you come back around to the place you started. Finish your floss at the back of the body (page 12).

Adding
FEET & FLIPPERS

Some of your Mini Animals will have feet or flippers that stick out. Here's an easy way to keep them from moving out of place while you stitch.

1 Lay the front body piece down and move the feet around under it, until you like they way they look.

2 Use black floss to make one small stitch through the base of the penguin body and through one foot.

3 Repeat Step 2 for the other foot, and finish your floss (page 12).

WILD
TIPS

Penguin feet look nice as a single layer of felt, but some flippers look best doubled up. For wings or ears, try cutting two pieces for each and stitching them together before you attach them to your mini animal.

Stuffing
& FINISHING

It's time to puff up that penguin with some stuffing! Cut open the stuffing bag, pull out a small bit, and pull it apart so it's nice and fluffy.

1 Put the penguin front (with feet) on top of the penguin back piece. Using two strands of black floss, begin to whip stitch the outside edges of your two body sides.

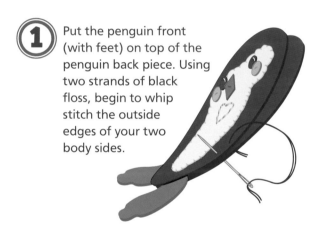

2 When you come to the first foot, switch to a straight stitch over the top of it. Your stitches should go through the front, the foot, and the back.

WILD
TIPS
Finish your floss on stitches at the back of your animals so the knots won't show from the front.

3 After you pass the foot, return to stitching around the fabric edge, then repeat Step 3 for the other foot.

4 Once you have only about 1 inch (2.5 cm) left of unstitched edges, begin adding stuffing to the penguin.

5 When you feel like your penguin is full enough, make the last few stitches to close it up. Finish your floss.

Adding Wings

Using the whip stitch (page 18), attach the wings to each side of your penguin.

I'm chill.

SLOTH

FIELD GUIDE

Supplies:
- Gray floss
- Black floss
- Cream floss

Trace and Cut:

 x2

2 sloth body

1 sloth face

 x2

2 eye markings

1 nose

FACE

1 Attach the eye markings and the nose with a whip stitch (page 18).

2 Use back stitch to create white eyes and a black mouth (page 16).

3 Attach the sloth face to one side of the sloth body using whip stitch.

ASSEMBLE

4 Attach the two body pieces together (wrong sides facing). Stop 1 inch (2.5 cm) before the end so you can stuff your sloth.

5 Once you've got it stuffed enough (not too much), continue stitching to close the gap, then finish your floss.

Take it slow…

22

BAT

FACE

1 Add a face to the bat front using black floss. You can add four tiny stitches in cream for fangs.

2 Use whip stitch to attach the bat front to one of the bat body pieces.

Let's hang out!

ASSEMBLE

3 Using a straight stitch, attach the ears and wings behind the front bat body (page 19).

4 Attach the two body pieces together (wrong sides facing). Stop 1 inch (2.5 cm) before the end so you can stuff the body.

FIELD GUIDE

Supplies:
- Black floss
- Cream floss

Trace and Cut:

x2

2 bat body

1 bat front

x2

x2

2 bat ears

2 bat wings

5 Once you've got it stuffed enough (not too much), finish the seam.

PIG

FACE

1 Make a snout by laying one circle on the pig body, and attaching it with two large stitches. These will be the nostrils of your pig.

2 Add eyes just above the snout for maximum cuteness.

ASSEMBLE

3 Cut one of the pig circles into a spiral to make the tail.

4 Attach the ears, feet, and tail using a small stitch for each.

5 Attach the two body pieces together (wrong sides facing). Stop 1 inch (2.5 cm) before the end so you can stuff the body.

I'm such a ham!

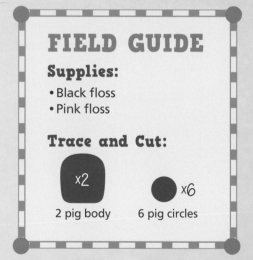

FIELD GUIDE

Supplies:
- Black floss
- Pink floss

Trace and Cut:

x2

2 pig body

x6

6 pig circles

6 Once you've got it stuffed enough (not too much), finish the seam.

7 Fold down the ears and make one small stitch in each to attach them just above the eyes.

WHALE

FACE & FINS

1 Add a face to one whale body piece.

2 Line up a fin with the top of one belly piece and stitch it in place. Repeat with the other fin and belly.

ASSEMBLE

3 Whip stitch the belly piece onto the front body piece using cream floss.

Repeat for the other body and belly pieces.

4 Use whip stitch to attach the two body and belly pieces together (wrong sides facing). Stop every so often, to put stuffing in the tail and body.

FIELD GUIDE

Supplies:
• Blue floss
• Cream floss

Trace and Cut:

x2   x2

2 whale body   2 whale fins

x2

2 whale bellies

Whale, hello there!

5 Once you've got it stuffed enough (not too much), then finish the seam.

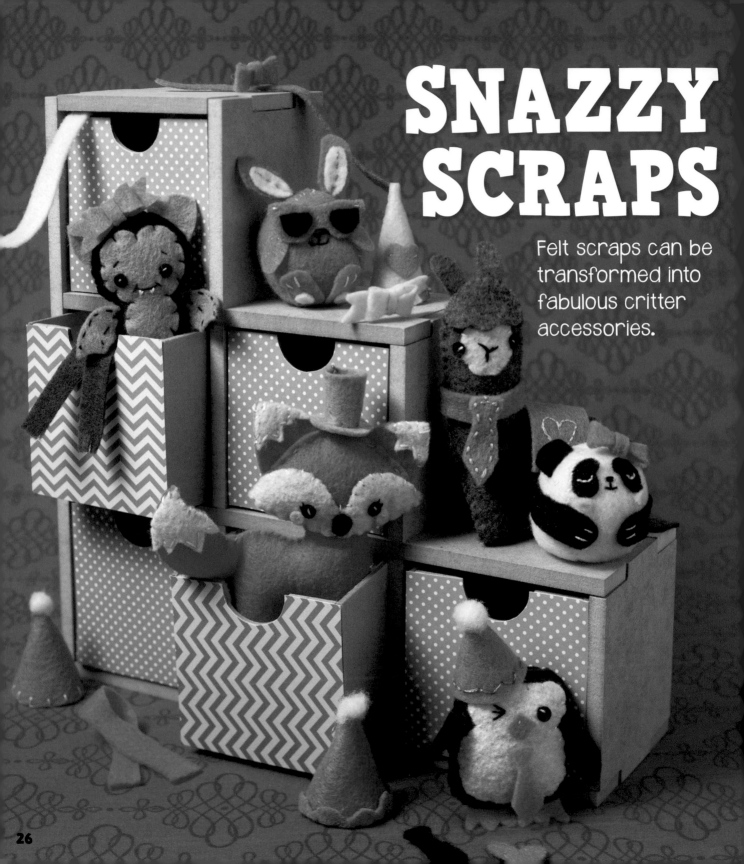

SNAZZY SCRAPS

Felt scraps can be transformed into fabulous critter accessories.

BOW

Try making some of these details to decorate your Mini Animals.

1 Take the bow center and fold it so the two edges meet. Then use a simple stitch to keep them together.

2 Use another simple stitch to attach the bow tail onto the back of the bow center you just folded.

3 Take the bow loop and fold it around the center and tail. Use a simple stitch at the back to hold the whole thing together, and finish your floss.

FIELD GUIDE

Supplies:
• Floss to match your bow

Trace and Cut:

1 bow tail   1 bow loop

1 bow center

Take a bow.

PARTY HAT

FIELD GUIDE

Supplies:

• Floss to match your hat

Trace and Cut:

1 party hat

 Roll the hat into a cone and stitch the sides together.

You can decorate it with felt shapes or add a fuzzy ball on top.

TOP HAT

1 Stitch together the edges of the top to make a tube.

FIELD GUIDE

Supplies:

• Floss to match your hat

Trace and Cut:

1 top hat top — 1 top hat bottom

2 Stitch the tube to the bottom in a couple of places.

FIELD GUIDE

Supplies:
- Cream floss
- Black floss

Cut:

1 pair of glasses

SUNGLASSES

1 Add one small stitch in cream on each corner of the glasses, as shown.

2 Attach the glasses to your felty friend by making a few stitches on the face.

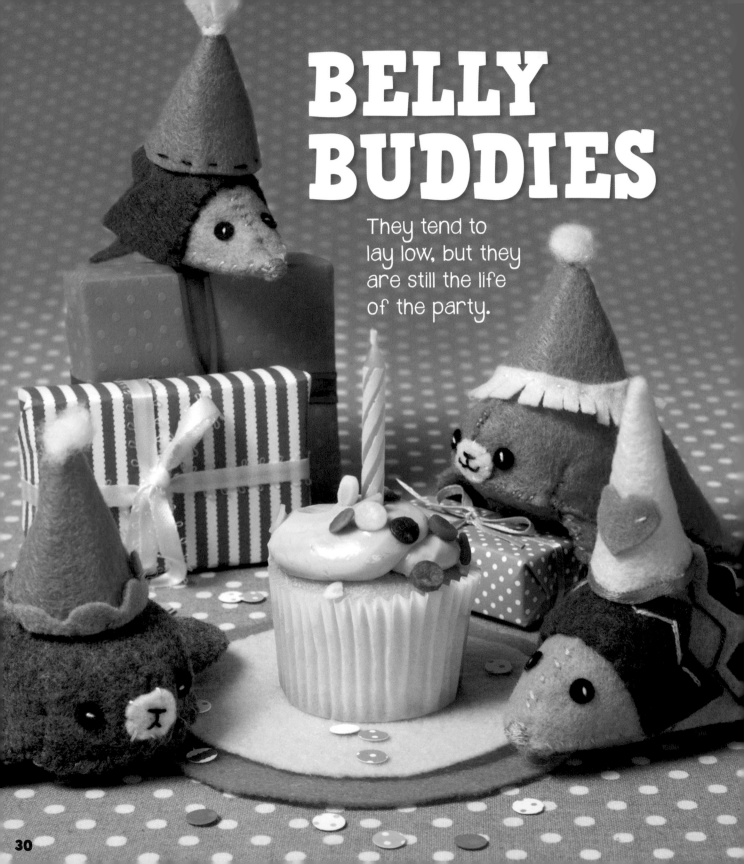

BELLY BUDDIES

They tend to lay low, but they are still the life of the party.

SEAL

FACE

 1 Using back stitch, make a nose and mouth on the face piece.

One stitch straight across, one down, and two diagonals make a cute face. You'll add the eyes later.

ASSEMBLE

 2 The little triangles that you cut out of the body pieces are called darts and they help make rounder shapes. Sew the edges of the dart together on one piece. Repeat on the other body piece.

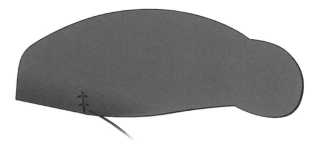

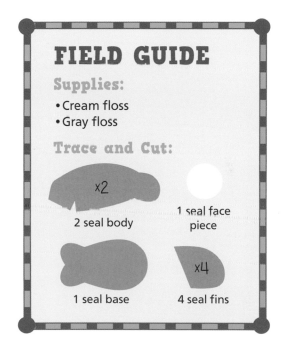

FIELD GUIDE

Supplies:
- Cream floss
- Gray floss

Trace and Cut:

x2

2 seal body

1 seal face piece

1 seal base

x4

4 seal fins

③ Attach the two body pieces together (wrong sides facing out).

④ Turn the body right side out, and using whip stitch, attach the face piece to the front of the seal body, near the bottom, as shown.

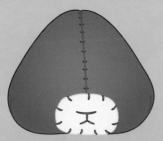

⑤ Attach the eyes just above the face piece.

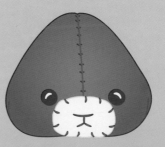

6 Take two of the fins and whip stitch them together. Repeat for the other set of fins.

7 Attach the fins to the body, just behind the darts one on each side.

8 Use whip stitch to attach the seal base to the seal body, stuff, then finish the seam.

You've got my seal of approval!

HEDGEHOG

BODY

1 Using whip stitch, attach the two body pieces together, right sides facing. Flip them right side out.

ASSEMBLE

2 Attach the eyes near the pointy end.

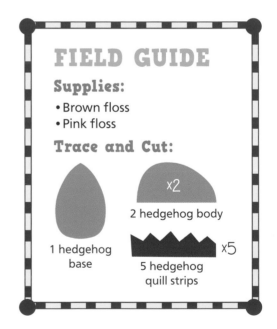

3 Use whip stitch to attach the hedgehog base to the seal body, stuff, then finish the seam.

QUILLS

4 Take one of the quill strips and find where it lines up to just touch the back of the hedgehog. Trim the edge of the strip on both sides, if needed.

FIELD GUIDE

Supplies:
- Brown floss
- Pink floss

Trace and Cut:

1 hedgehog base

x2
2 hedgehog body

x5
5 hedgehog quill strips

5 Use whip stitch to attach the strip to the body. Remember to keep the stitch loose enough so it doesn't pull the body and make it smaller.

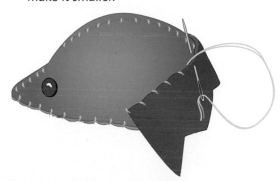

6 For the second strip of quills, lay it over the top of the first so that it just covers the whip stitching. Then sew it in place.

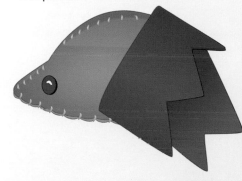

7 Repeat two more times, or until it you reach just behind the eyes, then use small stitches in pink to make a nose.

Looking sharp!

WILD
TIPS
Use different colored quill strips and decorative stitches for a unique look.

FOUR-LEGGED FRIENDS

These animals have legs that let them stand around a campfire, or decorate a shelf.

FOX

FIELD GUIDE

Supplies:
- Orange floss
- Cream floss

Trace and Cut:

 x2

2 fox body

1 fox legs

 1 fox face

 1 fox nose

x2
2 fox ears

x2
2 fox ear tips

1 fox tail tip

FACE

1 Attach the eyes, cheeks, and nose to the fox face.

2 Use whip stitch to attach the fox face to one body piece. This will be the front.

DETAILS

3 Use small stitches to attach the ear tips to the ears, and the tail tip to the front body piece.

ASSEMBLY

4 Whip stitch the top of the body pieces together with the right sides facing out. Start at the base of the tail and stop at the chest.

5 Stuff the head and tail, making sure to get some stuffing into the small corners.

6 Starting at the front, attach the legs piece using whip stitch.

7 Continue around the four legs, putting a little stuffing into each as you sew around it. Periodically check to make sure the legs and back that you haven't sewn yet still line up.

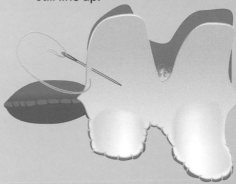

8 Just before you finish stitching, stuff a bit more into the fox, and then finish your seam.

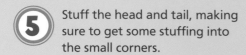

I'm pretty sly.

RACCOON

The Raccoon is made in almost the same way as the fox, with a few changes in felt colors and details.

FIELD GUIDE

Supplies:

- Gray floss
- Cream floss
- Black floss

Trace and Cut:

x2

2 fox body

1 fox legs

1 fox face

1 nose

x2
2 fox ears

x2
2 raccoon eye markings

x3
3 raccoon stripes

FACE

1 Attach the eye markings and nose to the raccoon face.

2 Use cream floss to stitch eyes on the eye markings.

3 Use whip stitch to attach the raccoon face to the front body piece.

DETAILS

4 Use simple stitches to attach the stripes to the raccoon tail on the front body piece.

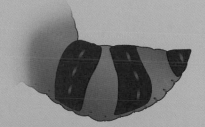

ASSEMBLY

5 Repeat Steps 4–8 of the fox instructions to finish the raccoon (pages 37-38). For smaller and rounder raccoon ears, pinch the base of the ear together before you stitch it in place.

ALPACA

FACE

1 Back stitch a Y shape onto the alpaca face. This will form the nose and mouth.

2 Whip stitch the face onto the right side of one alpaca body piece.

3 Attach the eyes so they just overlap the edge of the face on either side of the nose.

FIELD GUIDE

Supplies:
- Brown floss
- Black floss
- Cream floss

Trace and Cut:

x2

2 alpaca body   1 underside

1 alpaca face   1 alpaca hair   x2 2 alpaca ears

HEAD

4 Use simple stitches to attach the two ears to the back of the body piece, and the hair to the front. The hair should rest just above the eyes. If it's too long, you can trim it with scissors.

BODY

5 Use whip stitch to attach the tops of the two alpaca body pieces together. Start at the chest and continue to just under the tail.

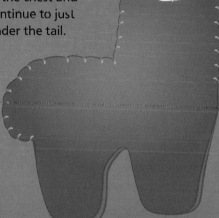

6 Attach the underside to the body and legs. See page 38, Steps 6–8.

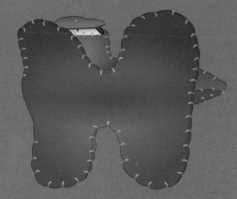

WILD TIPS

Add a bow (page 27), or a rectangle of felt as a blanket, to dress your alpaca for success.

All packed and ready to go!

CUTE ALL AROUND

These puffy stuffies will keep you in stitches.

BUNNY

FACE

 Add a face to one of the round body pieces. Put it slightly above center, as shown. Set this piece aside for now.

ASSEMBLE

 Take two of the other round body pieces and place them so the right sides are facing each other.

 Whip stitch the two pieces together along one edge.

FIELD GUIDE

Supplies:
- Pink floss
- Black floss
- Cream floss

Trace and Cut:

 x4

4 round body pieces

 x2

2 bun. arms

 x2

2 bunny ears

x2

2 bun. ears (2)

 x2

2 bunny feet

Now take the piece with the face and line it up with the free edge of one of the sewn pieces (eyes should be facing inside), then whip stitch those edges together.

 Take your final round body piece, and begin to attach it the same way you did in Step 4, but stop after just a couple of stitches.

 Flip the bunny body right side out.

44

Stuff the bunny through the open seam, then close it with whip stitch.

Ear-resistable!

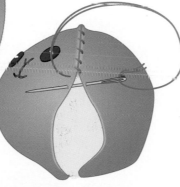

DETAILS

 To make the ears, use a couple of simple stitches to attach the cream center to the outside ear.

(9) Use a few simple stitches to attach the arms, feet, and ears to the bunny body.

WILD
STYLE
For an even more adorable bunny, add stitched details to the bunny's feet and ears before attaching them.

PANDA

FIELD GUIDE

Supplies:
- Black floss
- Cream floss

Trace and Cut:

 x4

4 round body pieces

 x2

2 panda eye markings

x2

2 panda ears

1 panda arm band

WILD
TIPS
Stitch some cream fingers on the arm band, or a little black "x" on the belly to cutify your critter.

FACE

1 Use black floss to back stitch a nose and mouth just above the center of the piece.

2 On each side of the mouth and nose, whip stitch the two panda eye markings.

3 Back stitch eyes on the eye markings in cream floss.

ASSEMBLE

4 Attach the body pieces, then stuff and close like you did for the bunny (see pages 43–45).

DETAILS

5 With black floss, use a few small stitches to attach the panda arm band to the panda body under the eye markings.

6 Use black floss to whip stitch the ears to the top.

OCTOPUS

FACE & BODY

1 Back stitch a mouth onto one body piece and attach or stitch some eyes and cheeks.

2 Attach the body pieces, then stuff and close like you did for the bunny (see pages 43–45).

LEGS

3 Use a couple of simple stitches to attach the legs to the bottom of the body.

WILD
TIPS
Use a different color for each body piece to make a colorful splash.

FIELD GUIDE

Supplies:
• Purple floss

Trace and Cut:

x4

4 round body pieces

1 octopus legs

Free hugs!

OWL

FIELD GUIDE

Supplies:
- Brown floss
- Orange floss

Trace and Cut:

x4
4 round body pieces

x2
2 owl wings

x2
2 owl circle (O1)

x2
2 owl ears

1 beak (B1)

1 owl belly

FACE & BODY

1 Find the owl circle pattern labeled "O1" on the pattern sheet. Cut out two of these in cream felt.

2 Lay an eye on each of the owl circles, and then stitch *both* to the brown body piece.

WILD TIPS
Stitches on the belly and wings will make your owl look even smarter.

3 Use some small stitches to attach a beak (B1) and owl belly as well.

4 Whip stitch the body pieces, then stuff and close like you did for the bunny (see pages 43–45).

DETAILS

5 Use whip stitch to attach the wings to the side of the body.

6 Pinch the base of one ear, and use a few whip stitches to hold it closed.

7 Repeat for the other ear, then attach them to the head and push them down.

This is a hoot!